STUDENTS CHOICE

Recreational Solos for

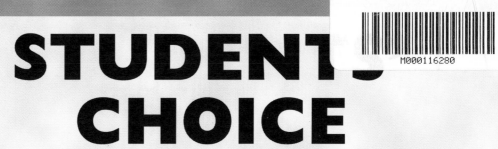

THE MUSIC TREE
PART 3

**Selected and Edited
by
Frances Clark
Louise Goss
Sam Holland**

Contents

Copyright © 2001 Summy-Birchard Music
Division of Summy-Birchard Inc.
All Rights Reserved   Printed in USA
ISBN 1-58951-004-6

Summy-Birchard Inc.
Exclusively distributed by
Warner Bros. Publications
15800 N.W. 48th Avenue
Miami, Florida 33014

Rag Man

Carefree, with bounce

Tony Caramia

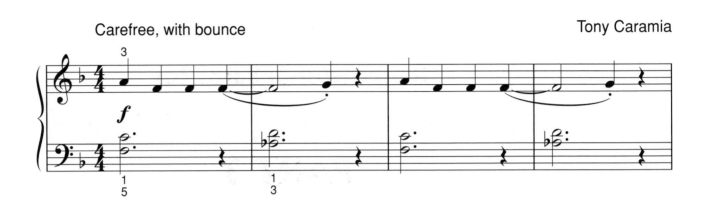

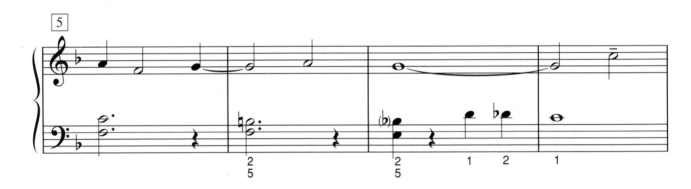

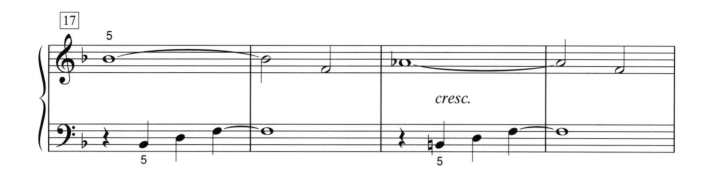

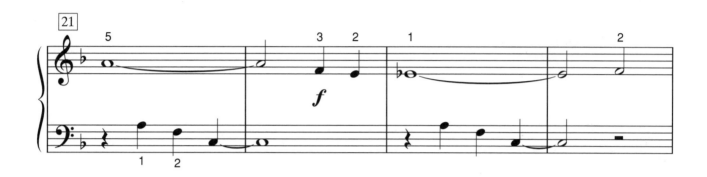

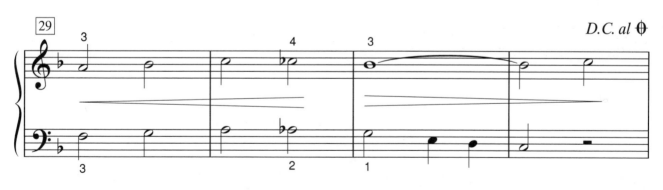

Distant Chimes

Dreamily

Jon George

damper pedal as marked
soft pedal throughout

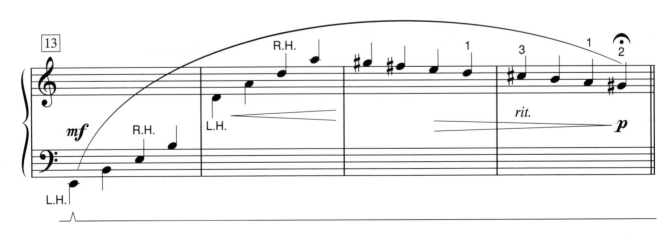

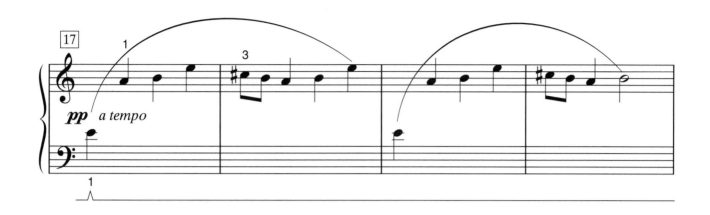

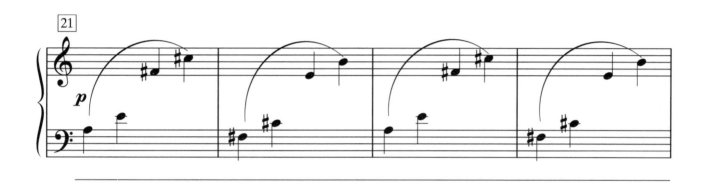

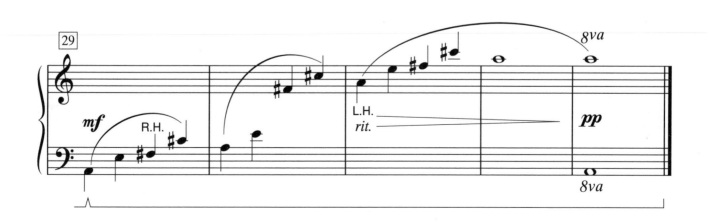

Pirates Bold

Boisterously

Marie Seuel Holst

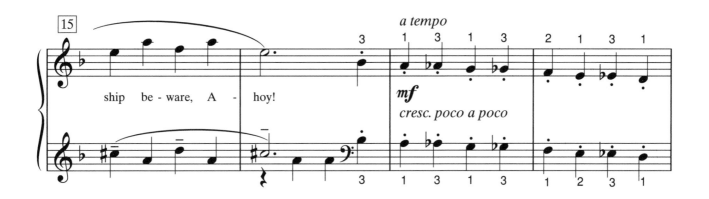

ship be - ware, A - hoy!

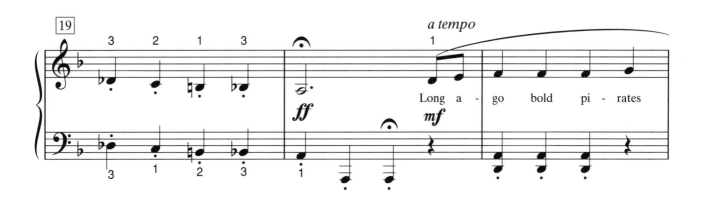

Long a - go bold pi - rates

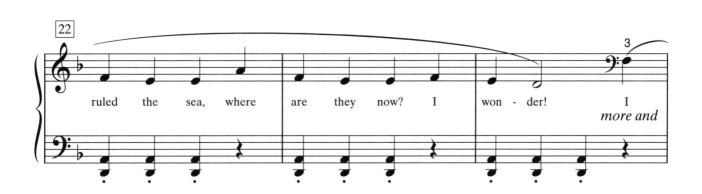

ruled the sea, where are they now? I won - der! I

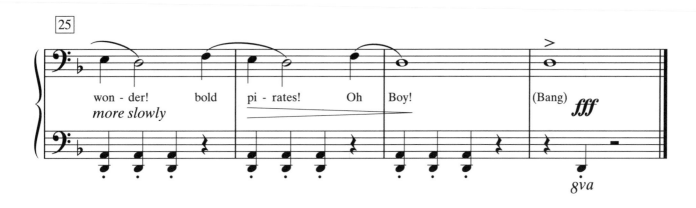

won - der! bold pi - rates! Oh Boy! (Bang)

Cowboy Blues

Lazily

Deborah Schwenk

ISBN 0-913277-28-2

Music Tree 3, pg. 35

8

Chattanooga Cha-Cha

Solidly

Jon George

Rock Ballad

Deep and smooth

Sam Holland

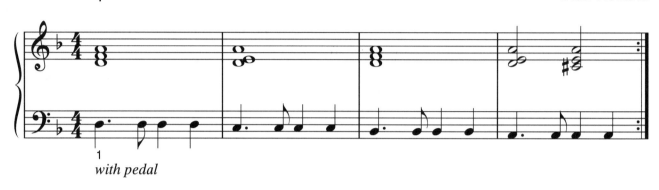

with pedal

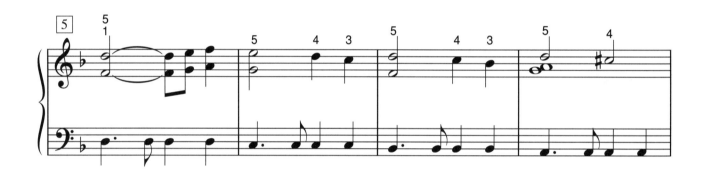

(octave optional)

Travelin' Man

Movin' on

Sam Holland

Night Clouds

Gently

Lynn Freeman Olson

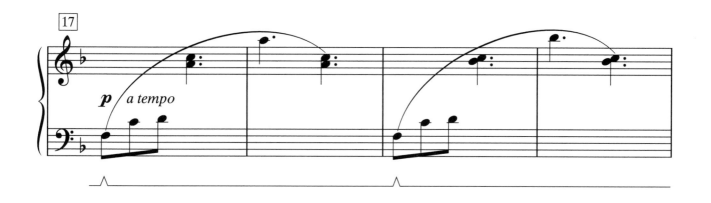

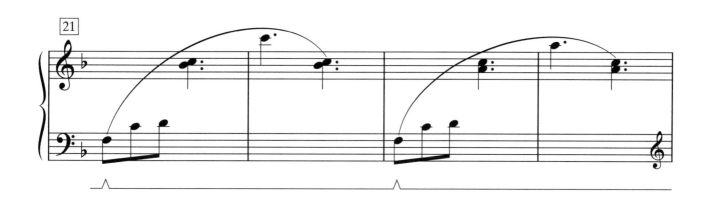

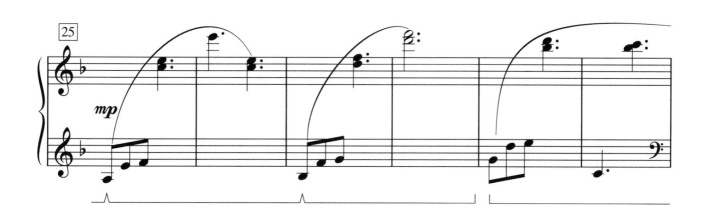

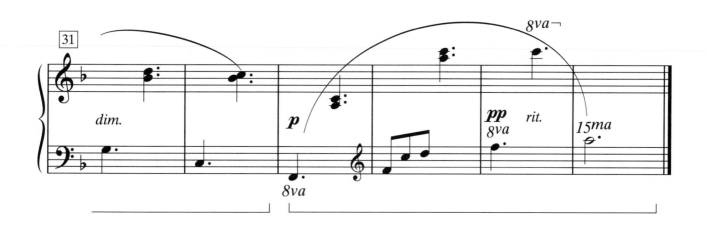

15

Bobo Boogies

Travelin'

Sam Holland

L.H. 8va throughout

A Song

Lyrical

Sam Holland

mp

with pedal

Fine
L.H. *over*

mf

D.C. al Fine

mf

Pagoda

Slowly, calmly

Lynn Freeman Olson

SUMCO 5853
ISBN 0-87487-803-9

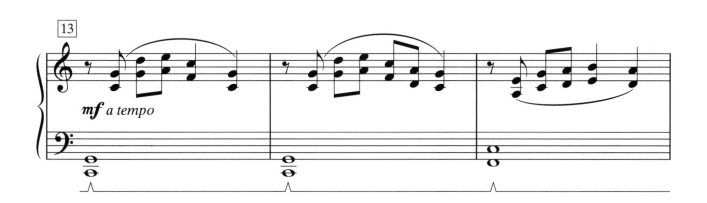

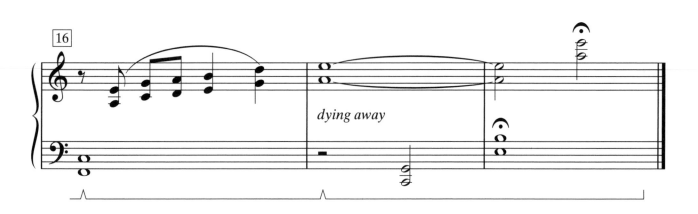

Rockin' Slow

Gently moving

Elvina Truman Pearce

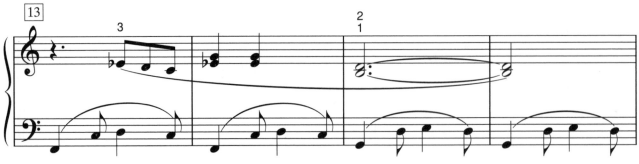

I'd Like to Teach the World to Sing
(in Perfect Harmony)

Words and Music by
B. BACKER, B. DAVIS,
R. COOK and R. GREENAWAY
Arranged by Sam Holland

Moderate swing

L.H. lightly staccato

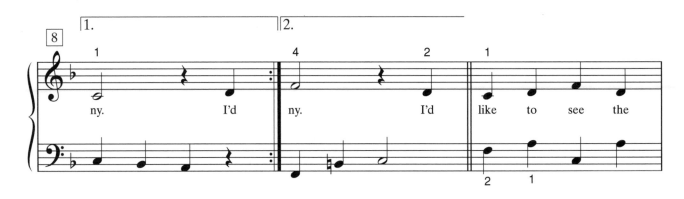

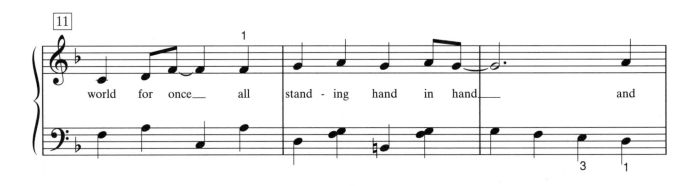

Music Tree 3, pg. 45

22

hear them ech - o through the hills___ for peace through - out the

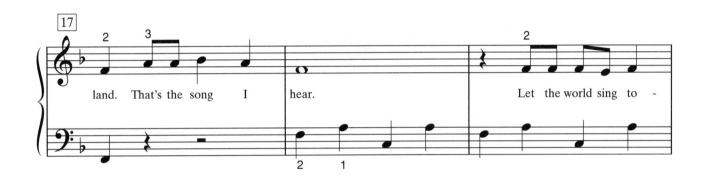

land. That's the song I hear. Let the world sing to -

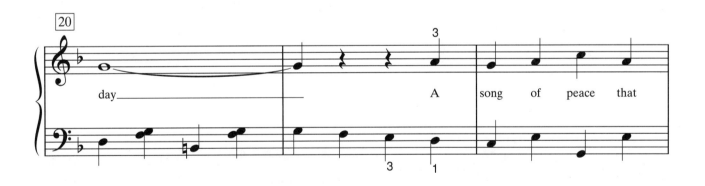

day_____ A song of peace that

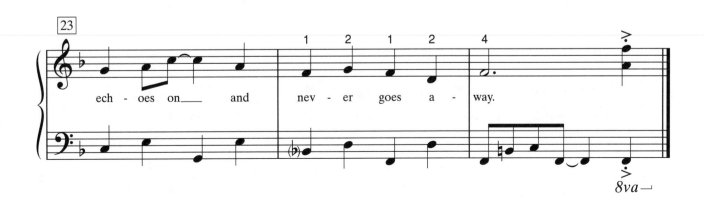

ech - oes on___ and nev - er goes a - way.

8va⌐

23

The Entertainer

Scott Joplin
Arranged by Sam Holland